GIN-SOAKED COCKTAILS AND CONCOCTIONS

JUNIPERLOOZA

ELOUISE ANDERS
ILLUSTRATIONS BY ANNA MANOLATOS

Smith
Street
Books

CONTENTS

INTRODUCTION

—

SHAKEN OR STIRRED, GIN IS THE FOUNDATION OF MANY OF OUR GREATEST COCKTAILS.

The Martini (page 25). The Negroni (page 21). The Gimlet (page 26). This botanical spirit has helped build many delicious drinks, as well as a history that's worth a read while you sip a Tom Collins (page 22).

Juniper berries and alcohol are fast friends, mixed for centuries, though the results weren't always as delicious as they are today. Tracing back to Italy in the 11th century, Benedictine monks mixed juniper and alcohol for medicinal purposes. Jump to 17th-century Netherlands and the combination had a new name: genever. Made by mixing malt wine and juniper berries, it still wasn't quite what you stir into your G&T. Then came the British soldiers.

A shortening of genever by British soldiers gave us gin, and gin gave England a new pastime. The alcohol swept the nation in the early 18th century, but not everyone was happy about it. This period is described as the Gin Craze, depicted in art as a collapse of society. Until the mid-1700s, the English were, as reports would have it, losing their

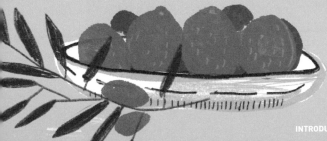

minds, and gin was the culprit. Its reputation took a turn for the infamous and, by the 1750s, the law managed to largely shut sales down. While gin didn't disappear, it did take a backseat until the 1800s.

Distillation technologies improved, and with them, the clarity of the liquor and its list of ingredients. Juniper stepped forward and turpentine stepped out. Dry gin (see page 9) appeared on the market, and British sailors started mixing it into their safeguard against malaria: tonic. Lime joined the party and mixology never looked back, creating a slew of classic cocktails that we now know and love to sip.

Like cocktails, gin took another backseat for a stretch of the 20th century, but both enjoyed a renaissance at the turn of the millennium. Today, there's a boom in gin distillers producing classic drys and modern twists that experiment

with new botanical blends, which is great news for the gin cocktail. While the martini is an indomitable feat, the floral, fruity and spicy gins on the market today have transformed old classics, invented new ones and are extremely sippable on their own.

This book is a distillation of gin past and present: the Martini (page 25) and vesper (page 51), the Southside (page 18) and Bramble (page 91). Pour a Bee's knees spritz (page 66), take a slice of a Cherry pie (page 104) and start the day with a Breakfast martini (page 107). Create new drinks with your own infusions and discover gin's botanical nuances with over 60 recipes.

Juniperlooza has everything you need to start your own gin craze, so chill your martini glasses, call some friends and mix your way through some very good cocktails.

TYPES OF GIN

—

Like vodka, gin is typically made with a neutral spirit created from distilling grains like wheat, corn or rye.

Juniper and other botanicals are added during distillation, creating a new, herbaceous liquor. Thanks to the recent gin renaissance, there's more distillers making more types of gin than ever, which is great news for lovers of the G&T, and bad news for anyone who is indecisive in stores. Traditional gins now sit on shelves alongside more modern, craft-focused creations that experiment with new flavours. If you're wondering which to buy, here's a quick rundown:

LONDON DRY

If you've had a martini, you've probably sampled London Dry gin.

'Dry' indicates that nothing but botanicals were added to the base spirit during production, and nothing was added after distillation beyond water. This style of gin appeared in the mid-1800s, when advances in distillation technology improved taste; gin no longer needed sweeteners for palatability.

Without sub-par distillation (and additions like sawdust) juniper was allowed to truly shine. While this style of gin is no longer solely produced in London, it is versatile and a safe bet for most cocktails. If you're going to stock one bottle of gin, grab a London Dry.

NEW WESTERN DRY

While juniper is still the star in this style of gin, it doesn't totally dominate the palate. Other botanicals are brought forward for a bigger supporting role, steering gin in a brand-new direction.

If you're feeling adventurous, these gins are a great option to put a spin on the classics, or to pair with new inventions. If you're shaking up something fruity or spiced, check out this section of the aisle.

GENEVER

Gin's Dutch predecessor, genever is produced with malted grains, which give impart a pronounced flavour to the alcohol. Juniper is present, but it's not the star of the show. Genever is less botanical and more malty, which means that it doesn't suit just any gin cocktail.

If you'd like to sample genever, leave it out of your Tom Collins (page 22) and try it in something full-bodied like a Negroni (page 21).

OLD TOM

The rise of London Dry led to Old Tom's historical decline. Harkening back to the days of bad-tasting gin, Old Tom featured sweeteners to make things more palatable. The arrival of dry gin pushed its sweetened predecessor off shelves and out of popular favour. By the mid-20th century, Old Tom disappeared completely.

Fear not, however. Modern-day distillers have resurrected this style of gin.

Old Tom is sweeter than dry options, but it's still a far cry from a syrupy liqueur. This richer style of gin tastes great in drinks invented in the 1800s and early 1900s, when the original Old Tom was still in use, like the Collins (page 22) or the Martinez (page 34). When you're mixing historical cocktails, give Old Tom a try.

COMPOUND

Also called 'bathtub gin'. While that might not sound delicious, the name harkens back to the Prohibition, when alcohol production had to happen in secret. Unlike other gins, which are distilled with botanicals, compound gin is an infusion – juniper berries and other additions are left to steep in a neutral spirit, which infuses it with flavour.

You can make compound gin in your very own bathtub, or in the kitchen (page 134). All you need is a neutral spirit like vodka and botanicals of your choice.

NOTES ON INFUSIONS

—

It's easy to pop into the store to pick up a bottle of flavoured gin, but infusing is easy, and the payoff is delicious.

Some infusions take only hours, some a few days. Sloe gin (page 122) suits its name in more than one way: sloe berries are left to infuse for months, resulting in a rich liqueur. The wait is long, but if you have a cool, dark place to store a bottle, you can pretty much leave the berries and gin to work their magic.

Most recipes take far less time, but infusing is a choose-your-own adventure. Whether you'd like a blush of flavour or something stronger, the choice is yours.

Tweak infusion times to suit your preference and explore flavour options. Whether you want sweet or spicy, fruity or bitter, there's a wide world of ingredients to experiment with.

Juniperlooza includes a set of recipes for infusions, but don't be afraid to get creative. Swap ingredients, add new ones and explore how different aromatics interact with your gin. Along the way, you'll discover some delicious new spirits that you can mix into this book's cocktails.

To infuse gin, you need little equipment or expertise. Getting started at home is so easy, there are just a few basic tips to remember:

1

Don't use your best bottle of gin. Instead, try a mid-range pick.

2

Jars or containers used for infusing should be washed with hot, soapy water and dried before use.

3

Since most of the bottles that spirits come in have a small opening, you'll need to infuse in a different container – canning or mason jars work well and come with a handy lid.

4

Choose the correct size jar or container for the amount you are planning to make – this book's infusion recipes can be easily scaled up or down to suit your needs.

5

Aim to fill jars almost completely, so that any fresh ingredients are fully submerged.

6

When you are happy with your infusion, strain the liquid through a sieve lined with muslin (cheesecloth) into a clean jug to remove any solids or sediment.

7

Once you've made your infusion, you can store it in the bottle it came in; just remember to add a label to avoid any mix-ups and store in a cool, dark place for the longest shelf life. Infused spirits can be stored for up to a year.

THE CLASSICS

AVIATION

—

SERVES 1

A touch of crème de violette makes this drink bloom into an easily identifiable purple. If you don't want to hunt for the floral liqueur, you can go without. The results will still make your palate take flight, but the original's unique blend of cherries with violet and gin is worth the effort of recreating.

INGREDIENTS

...

ice cubes

60 ml (¼ cup) gin

1 tablespoon lemon juice

2 teaspoons maraschino liqueur

1 tablespoon crème de violette

washed violets, to garnish

lemon twist, to garnish

HOW TO

...

Fill a cocktail shaker with ice and add the gin, lemon juice, maraschino liqueur and crème de violette. Shake for 30 seconds until well combined, then strain into a chilled cocktail glass.

Garnish with violets and a lemon twist.

CLOVER CLUB

—

SERVES 1

In some drinks, the fruit overpowers the other ingredients. Not in the clover club. The raspberry syrup is a balanced touch that lends gin just the right level of sweetness. Paired with a foamy head, the results are a favourite of modern mixologists who rediscovered this drink during the cocktail revival of the 90s to early 2000s.

INGREDIENTS
...

60 ml (¼ cup) Raspberry gin (page 138)

20 ml (¾ fl oz) Raspberry syrup (page 144)

20 ml (¾ fl oz) lemon juice

1 egg white or 30 ml (1 fl oz) aquafaba

ice cubes

3 raspberries, to garnish

HOW TO
...

Pour the gin, raspberry syrup, lemon juice and egg white or aquafaba into a cocktail shaker and dry shake for 15 seconds. Add ice and shake for another 15 seconds.

Strain into a chilled coupe. Thread the raspberries onto a cocktail stick and sit across the top of the glass.

SOUTHSIDE

—

SERVES 1

A drink with muddled origins and mint. Wherever the southside emerged from, its winning combination of gin, mint and citrus firmly earned it a place as a cocktail classic. Fans of mojitos or gimlets will enjoy this southern cousin.

INGREDIENTS
•••

7 mint leaves, plus a sprig to garnish

60 ml (¼ cup) gin

1 tablespoon lemon juice

1 tablespoon lime juice

ice cubes

HOW TO
•••

Place the mint leaves in a cocktail shaker and gently muddle. Add the gin, lemon juice, lime juice and ice, and shake for 30 seconds until well combined.

Strain into a chilled cocktail glass and serve garnished with a mint sprig.

NEGRONI

—

SERVES 1

SERVES 1

The negroni started its life as an Americano, but it lacked one key ingredient: gin. Thankfully, that was rectified in the 20th century when sparkling water was swapped with the liquor. The result? A drink that's launched plenty of variations, perhaps none of which quite match the original's delicious bitterness.

INGREDIENTS
...

25 ml (¾ fl oz) gin

25 ml (¾ fl oz) sweet vermouth

25 ml (¾ fl oz) Campari

ice cubes

orange twist, to garnish

HOW TO
...

Pour the gin, vermouth and Campari into a mixing glass filled with ice, and stir until cold.

Add ice to a rocks glass. Pour over the mixed spirits, and garnish with an orange twist.

TOM COLLINS

—

SERVES 1

The Tom Collins requires no bartending finesse. A quick shake and you have a classic, no elusive ingredients required. Served in a taller glass, this drink is a great option for gin lovers who want their drink to last, or for those who want to feel a little less buzzed by the time they find the bottom.

INGREDIENTS
...

4–5 ice cubes

60 ml (¼ cup) gin

20 ml (¾ fl oz) lemon juice

1 tablespoon Sugar syrup (page 143)

chilled sparkling water, to top

lemon wheel and 2 maraschino cherries
on a cocktail stick, to garnish

HOW TO
...

Place the ice cubes in a Collins glass. Add the gin, lemon juice and sugar syrup to the glass and use a long-stemmed spoon to mix well.

Top with sparkling water and garnish with the lemon wheel and maraschino cherries.

MARTINI

—

SERVES 1

There's nothing that feels quite as elegant as an evening with a martini in hand. This recipe produces a deliciously dry drink; if you want to get wet, swap your ratios and increase the vermouth. Whichever you choose, more than two martinis and the drink may start to feel a little less refined.

INGREDIENTS
...

60 ml (¼ cup) gin

1 tablespoon dry vermouth

ice cubes

3 olives on a cocktail stick, to garnish

HOW TO
...

Pour the gin and vermouth into a mixing glass filled with ice and stir until cold. Strain into a chilled martini glass.

Garnish with the olives.

GIMLET

—

SERVES 1

If you're looking to avoid scurvy, the gimlet was a favourite method of British sailors. If you're just looking for a great cocktail, it's also a good solution. Tradition on the high seas dictates that the gimlet is built with lime cordial, not juice. If you have a bottle at the ready, you can skip preparing the syrup.

INGREDIENTS
•••

ice cubes

60 ml (¼ cup) gin

20 ml (¾ fl oz) Lime syrup (page 144)

squeeze of lime juice

lime wheel, to garnish

HOW TO
•••

Fill a cocktail shaker with ice, then add the gin and lime syrup and juice. Shake for 30 seconds, until well combined, then strain into a chilled cocktail glass.

Serve garnished with a lime wheel.

GIN RICKEY

—

SERVES 1

A cocktail with a name that belies its age, the gin rickey was created in the 19th century. If you lack a sweet tooth, this is the drink for you. With no sugar in sight, the rickey relies on a tried and trusted pairing: gin and lime. To make the drink your own, experiment with different gins. With the rickey, you can't go wrong.

INGREDIENTS
...

ice cubes

60 ml (¼ cup) gin

20 ml (¾ fl oz) lime juice

chilled sparkling water, to top

3 lime wheels, to garnish

HOW TO
...

Fill a tall glass with ice and add the gin and lime juice.
Stir well to combine, then top with sparkling water.

Serve garnished with the lime wheels.

GIN FIZZ

—

SERVES 1

When you're always left wanting more after finishing a sour, try a fizz. The difference? Sparkling water and a taller glass. If that sounds like a Collins (page 22), you aren't mistaken. The main difference is the fizz's lack of ice. Add an egg (though it's not necessary), and you have a fizz. Add gin, and you have this drink.

INGREDIENTS
...

60 ml (¼ cup) gin

25 ml (¾ fl oz) lemon juice

1 tablespoon Sugar syrup (page 143)

1 egg white or 30 ml (1 fl oz) aquafaba (optional)

ice cubes

chilled sparkling water, to top

lemon twist, to garnish

HOW TO
...

Add the gin, lemon juice, sugar syrup and egg white or aquafaba (if using) to a cocktail shaker. If using egg or aquafaba, dry shake for 15 seconds, then add ice and shake for a further 15 seconds. Otherwise, add ice right away and shake for 30 seconds. Strain into a tall glass.

Top with sparkling water and garnish with a lemon twist.

THE LAST WORD

—

SERVES 1

*The last word may have you struggling to speak after
a couple, with an alcohol-laden list of ingredients. This
cocktail's reputation has carried it through the ages; a sip,
and it's easy to understand the fuss. Perfectly tangy, with
just the right amount of sweet, this heady green concoction
is a perfectly balanced way to lose an evening.*

INGREDIENTS
•••

20 ml (¾ fl oz) gin

20 ml (¾ fl oz) green chartreuse

20 ml (¾ fl oz) maraschino liqueur

20 ml (¾ fl oz) lime juice

2 Luxardo maraschino cherries
on a cocktail stick, to garnish

ice cubes

HOW TO
•••

Pour the gin, chartreuse, maraschino liqueur and lime juice
into a cocktail shaker filled with ice. Shake for 30 seconds,
until well combined.

Strain into a chilled coupe and garnish with the prepared
cocktail stick.

.

MARTINEZ

—

SERVES 1

Love a Martini (page 25)? A Manhattan? Raise a glass to their forebear: the Martinez. Sweeter than either, thanks to maraschino liqueur, this rich cocktail mixes herbal notes with cherry. For true fans of the fruit, you can use Cherry gin (page 126) and add maraschino cherries as a garnish.

INGREDIENTS

...

60 ml (¼ cup) gin

30 ml (1 fl oz) sweet vermouth

2 teaspoons maraschino liqueur

2 dashes of Angostura bitters

ice cubes

orange twist, to garnish

HOW TO

...

Add the gin, sweet vermouth, maraschino liqueur and bitters to a mixing glass filled with ice, and stir until cold. Strain into a chilled cocktail glass.

Serve garnished with an orange twist.

SINGAPORE SLING

—

SERVES 1

A long list of ingredients is easy to balk at when there are plenty of simpler drinks out there. The Singapore sling is worth the extra effort. Made correctly, it's a fruity, complex drink that captures mixology at its playful best, combining ingredients to great effect.

INGREDIENTS

•••

45 ml (1½ fl oz) gin

20 ml (¾ fl oz) cherry brandy

20 ml (¾ fl oz) Grand Marnier

2 teaspoons Bénédictine liqueur

30 ml (1 fl oz) pineapple juice

2 teaspoons lime juice

2 dashes of orange bitters

ice cubes

chilled sparkling water, to top

2 maraschino cherries, to garnish

orange wheel, to garnish

HOW TO

•••

Add the alcohols, juices and bitters to a cocktail shaker filled with ice. Shake vigorously for 30 seconds, then strain into a tall glass filled with ice. Top with sparkling water. Thread the maraschino cherries and an orange wheel onto a cocktail stick and sit it across the top of the glass.

GIBSON

—

SERVES 1

The absence of bitters used to define a Gibson from a dry martini. The main difference today? The garnish. If you order a martini, you may get an olive or maybe a lemon twist. Order a Gibson and your glass will arrive with a pickled onion, infusing the alcohol with a hint of umami.

INGREDIENTS
...

60 ml (¼ cup) gin

1 teaspoon dry vermouth

ice cubes

2 cocktail onions, to garnish

HOW TO
...

Add the gin and vermouth to a mixing glass filled with ice, shake for 30 seconds, then strain into a chilled cocktail glass.

Thread the onions onto a cocktail stick and add to the glass.

CORPSE REVIVER NO. 2

—

SERVES 1

A drink for the dead, or those nearly there. With enough liquor to give the system a jolt, this drink is part of the centuries-old tradition of chasing the hair of the dog. Lillet blanc replaces kina lillet from the 1930s recipe, as it's no longer available. For an even more modern twist, sub out the triple sec for yellow chartreuse.

INGREDIENTS
...

ice cubes

30 ml (1 fl oz) gin

30 ml (1 fl oz) triple sec

30 ml (1 fl oz) lillet blanc

30 ml (1 fl oz) lemon juice

1 dash of absinthe

orange twist, to garnish

HOW TO
...

In a cocktail shaker filled with ice, add the gin, triple sec, lillet blanc, lemon juice and absinthe. Shake for 30 seconds, then strain into a chilled coupe.

Garnish with an orange twist.

WHITE NEGRONI

—

SERVES 1

Although it's called a white negroni, this floral drink often takes on a yellow hue thanks to the inclusion of Suze. For the uninitiated, this French liqueur has a wide range of tasting notes that make it hard to describe. Earthy and vegetal, bitter and sweet, floral and citrusy. Sit with it, and it'll grow on you, particularly when paired with gin and lillet blanc.

INGREDIENTS
...

ice cubes, plus 1 large cube to garnish

40 ml (1¼ fl oz) gin

30 ml (1 fl oz) lillet blanc

30 ml (1 fl oz) Suze (or similar gentian-based liqueur)

washed nasturtium, to garnish

HOW TO
...

Fill a mixing glass with ice and add the gin, lillet blanc and Suze. Stir until cold.

Place a large ice cube in a rocks glass and pour over the mixed spirits. Serve garnished with a nasturtium.

ROSE MARTINI

ROSE MARTINI

—

SERVES 1

If you find a classic martini too alcoholic in taste, try adding rose petal syrup. This floral touch pairs wonderfully with a gin-forward martini. A few drops of orange bitters round off this drink's layers of flavour. Left-over syrup can find its way into a Rosewater fizz (page 77), or a glass of sparkling water.

INGREDIENTS
...

ice cubes

50 ml (1¾ fl oz) gin

20 ml (¾ fl oz) dry vermouth

2 teaspoons Rose petal syrup (page 145)

2–3 dashes of orange bitters

washed rose petal, to garnish

HOW TO
...

Fill a cocktail shaker with ice and add the gin, vermouth and rose petal syrup. Shake well for 30 seconds, then strain into a chilled martini glass.

Top with a few dashes of orange bitters and garnish with a rose petal.

TOM COLLINS BLUE

—

SERVES 1

A good cocktail is made with an eye to presentation, and this Tom Collins doesn't fail to deliver. With a touch of magic (and some acid from a lemon), the blue gin turns purple in a bartending trick that'll impress any guest. Better yet, this Collins tastes as good as it looks.

INGREDIENTS
...

4–5 ice cubes

60 ml (¼ cup) Blue floral gin (page 118)

20 ml (¾ fl oz) lemon juice

1 tablespoon Sugar syrup (page 143)

chilled sparkling water, to top

lemon wheel, to garnish

2 maraschino cherries on a cocktail stick, to garnish

HOW TO
...

Place the ice cubes in a Collins glass. Add the gin, lemon juice and sugar syrup, then use a long-stemmed spoon to mix well.

Top with sparkling water and garnish with a lemon wheel and the maraschino cherries.

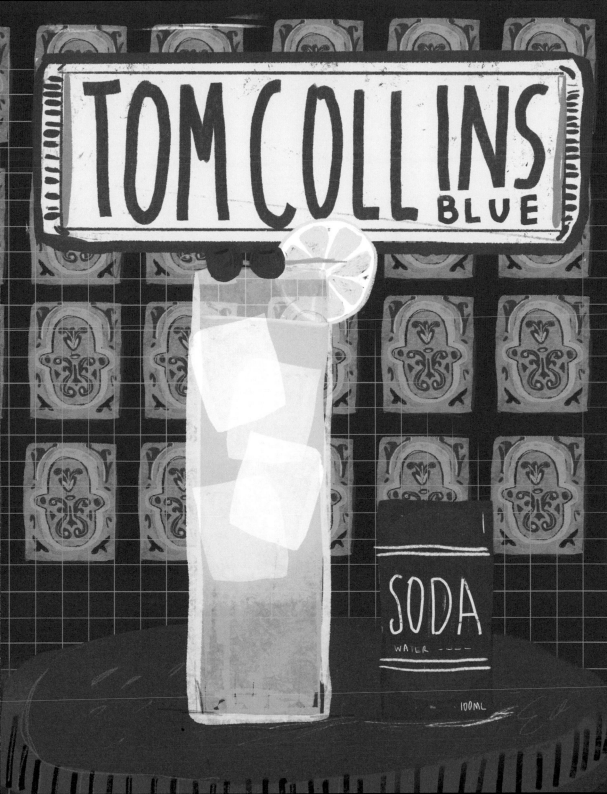

PEAR & VANILLA VESPER

—

SERVES 1

*When Bond orders a martini shaken, not stirred, he is asking for a vesper – inventing it, to be exact. Author Ian Fleming brought Bond and the vesper into creation in **Casino Royale**. His recipe adds vodka and swaps vermouth with kina lillet. Modern recipes swap the latter with lillet blanc. This recipe goes further with an infused gin to complement the lillet's notes of fruit.*

INGREDIENTS
...

90 ml (3 fl oz) Vanilla & pear gin (page 125)

30 ml (1 fl oz) vodka

1 tablespoon lillet blanc

lemon twist, to garnish

HOW TO
...

Pour the gin, vodka and lillet blanc into a cocktail shaker filled with ice, and shake for 15 seconds.

Strain into a chilled cocktail glass and garnish with a lemon twist.

ROSEMARY GIMLET

—

SERVES 1

Rosemary finds its way into dishes more than cocktail glasses, but it pairs beautifully with plenty of drinks, particularly the citrus-forward. While the traditional gimlet is perfect in its simplicity, a touch of rosemary syrup adds a herbal depth that'll soothe drinkers from the first sip to the last.

INGREDIENTS
...

60 ml (¼ cup) gin

30 ml (1 fl oz) lime juice

1 tablespoon Rosemary syrup (page 148)

ice cubes

rosemary sprig, to garnish

HOW TO
...

Pour the gin, lime juice and rosemary syrup into a cocktail shaker filled with ice. Shake well for 30 seconds, then strain into a chilled cocktail glass.

Garnish with a rosemary sprig.

Rosemary
GIMLET

LILAC FRENCH 75

—

SERVES 1

A gentle twist on a potent classic. Lilac's citrus notes pair with the 75's lemon juice for a fresh and floral glass that has a pleasant amount of sweetness. Lilac can taste bitter when eaten raw, but infused into syrup, the blooms mellow into a more subtle addition. If you already have Lavender syrup (page 147), you can swap that in for a Provençal version.

INGREDIENTS
...

ice cubes

30 ml (1 fl oz) gin

1 tablespoon lemon juice

1 tablespoon Lilac syrup (page 146)

chilled Champagne, to top

lemon twist, to garnish

washed lilac florets, to garnish

HOW TO
...

Fill a cocktail shaker with ice and add the gin, lemon juice and lilac syrup. Shake vigorously for 30 seconds, then strain into a champagne flute.

Top with Champagne and garnish with a lemon twist and lilac florets.

RUBY NEGRONI

—

SERVES 1

A departure from the original, this twist introduces raspberry through both gin and syrup, placing it at the forefront of the palate. Negroni fans will also note there's no vermouth. Port is used instead, its notes of berries complementing the other ingredients for a rich, ruby-hued experience.

INGREDIENTS

•••

ice cubes

25 ml (¾ fl oz) gin

1 tablespoon Campari

1 tablespoon port

1 teaspoon Raspberry syrup (page 144)

90 ml (3 fl oz) chilled sparkling white wine

2 raspberries, to garnish

orange twist, to garnish

HOW TO

•••

Fill a cocktail shaker with ice and add the gin, Campari, port and raspberry syrup. Shake for 30 seconds until well combined, then strain into a tumbler.

Top with the sparkling wine and garnish with the raspberries and an orange twist.

JASMINE WHITE LADY

—

SERVES 1

The classic white lady is a simple but very effective blend of orange liqueur, lemon juice and gin, finished off with a foamy froth of egg white: a silky, tart tipple. While delicious without alteration, lacing the drink with jasmine elevates the drink with a springtime aroma.

INGREDIENTS
•••

1 jasmine teabag or 1 teaspoon loose jasmine tea

125 ml (½ cup) near-boiling water

50 ml (1¾ fl oz) gin

25 ml (¾ fl oz) orange liqueur

2 teaspoons lemon juice

2 teaspoons Sugar syrup (page 143)

1 tablespoon egg white or aquafaba

ice cubes

HOW TO
•••

Combine the teabag or loose tea and water in a teapot. Steep for 3–4 minutes, then strain into a heatproof container and discard the teabag or loose tea. Refrigerate until cold.

Add the gin, orange liqueur, lemon juice, sugar syrup, egg white or aquafaba and 2 teaspoons of the jasmine tea to a cocktail shaker. Dry shake for 15 seconds, then add ice and shake for a further 15 seconds. Strain into a chilled cocktail glass.

SLOEGRONI

—

SERVES 1

The best way to improve on the Negroni (page 21)? Add more gin. Of course, Sloe gin (page 122) is technically a liqueur, infused with berries. Sweeter than its parts, it's a warm, plummy addition to the traditionally bitter cocktail. Some sloegronis swap the liqueur in for the gin or vermouth; this recipe just pours it on top. The more, the merrier.

INGREDIENTS
...

25 ml (¾ fl oz) gin

25 ml (¾ fl oz) Sloe gin (page 122)

25 ml (¾ fl oz) sweet vermouth

25 ml (¾ fl oz) Campari

ice cubes, plus 1 large cube to garnish

orange twist, to garnish

HOW TO
...

Pour the gin, sloe gin, vermouth and Campari into a mixing glass filled with ice, and stir until cold.

Place a large ice cube in a rocks glass and pour over the mixed spirits. Serve garnished with an orange twist.

SLOEGRONI

CAMPARI

BEE STING

—

SERVES 1

To spice things up, try this bee's knees with chilli-infused Honey syrup (page 143). The addition gives the citrus a kick, with just enough sweet heat to complement the original. If you don't want to infuse your own honey, head to the supermarket or deli for a bottle of ready-made hot honey; just make sure to dilute it into a syrup before adding any to a cocktail shaker.

INGREDIENTS
...

60 ml (¼ cup) gin

25 ml (¾ fl oz) lemon juice

30 ml (1 fl oz) hot Honey syrup (page 143)

ice cubes

lemon twist, to garnish

HOW TO
...

Add the gin, lemon juice and hot honey syrup to a cocktail shaker filled with ice. Shake for 30 seconds until well combined, and strain into a chilled coupe.

Garnish with a lemon twist.

THE BEE'S KNEES

—

SERVES 1

Cut a rug and down this spritz, inspired by the Prohibition-era classic. For those with a sweet tooth, the bee's knees' inclusion of honey is a welcome touch, adding just the right amount of richness. If you're tempted to mix honey straight from the bottle, a word of warning: it mixes better when it's diluted into a syrup.

INGREDIENTS
...

20 ml (¾ fl oz) Honey syrup (page 143)

50 ml (1¾ fl oz) gin

30 ml (1 fl oz) lemon juice

ice cubes

chilled sparkling white wine, to top

lemon twist, to garnish

HOW TO
...

Pour the honey syrup, gin and lemon juice into a cocktail shaker filled with ice. Shake vigorously for 30 seconds, then strain into a chilled coupe.

Top with sparkling wine and serve garnished with a lemon twist.

FRENCH 75

—

Taking its name from a gun, this potent combination of gin and Champagne is known to throw drinkers back. Finessed through the decades, the contemporary version is simple but delicious. Little work goes into mixing a French 75, but there's plenty of payoff from this glass of effervescent gin.

INGREDIENTS
...

ice cubes

60 ml (¼ cup) gin

30 ml (1 fl oz) Sugar syrup (page 143)

30 ml (1 fl oz) lemon juice

chilled Champagne, to top

lemon twist, to garnish

HOW TO
...

Fill a cocktail shaker with ice and add the gin, sugar syrup and lemon juice. Shake for 30 seconds, then strain into a champagne flute.

Top with Champagne and garnish with a lemon twist.

MONTE CARLO IMPERIAL

—

SERVES 1

There's no gamble here: the Monte Carlo imperial is a great cocktail. Featuring crème de menthe, this sweet, minty drink is the perfect end to a meal. If you love peppermint and you love bubbles, it's well worth trying a glass (or two).

INGREDIENTS
•••

ice cubes

45 ml (1½ fl oz) gin

20 ml (¾ fl oz) crème de menthe

20 ml (¾ fl oz) lemon juice

chilled Champagne, to top

mint leaf, to garnish

lemon twist, to garnish

HOW TO
•••

Fill a cocktail shaker with ice and add the gin, crème de menthe and lemon juice. Shake for 30 seconds until well combined, then strain into a tumbler and top with Champagne.

Garnish with a mint leaf and a lemon twist.

THE VALENCIA

—

SERVES 1

If the mimosa has you yawning, try the valencia at brunch. Introducing gin and vodka into the mix, it's a bit less sedate than the traditional glass of bubbles and OJ. To stay true to the Spanish original, make sure to use valencia oranges and Cava. In a pinch, these can be swapped with other oranges or bubbles that you already have in your kitchen.

INGREDIENTS
•••

20 ml (¾ fl oz) Citrus gin (page 137)

20 ml (¾ fl oz) vodka

45 ml (1½ fl oz) orange juice

chilled Cava, to top

ice cubes

orange wheel, to garnish

HOW TO
•••

Combine the gin, vodka, orange juice and Cava in a champagne flute. Stir and fill with ice.

Serve garnished with an orange wheel.

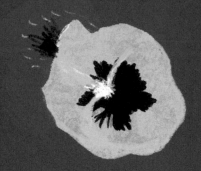

PANSY SPRITZ

—

SERVES 1

Roses may get the spotlight, but pansies are another traditional symbol of love. Share this spritz with a significant other or crush you want to impress. Great cocktails don't need to be complicated, and floral concoctions are a simple way to mix an interesting drink sure to win any heart.

INGREDIENTS
...

30 ml (1 fl oz) gin

30 ml (1 fl oz) pear juice

2 teaspoons Pansy syrup (page 146)

ice cubes

chilled Champagne, to top

washed pansy, to garnish

HOW TO
...

Add the gin, pear juice and pansy syrup to a cocktail shaker filled with ice. Shake for 15 seconds, then pour into a champagne flute.

Top with Champagne and serve garnished with a pansy.

CHAMPAGNE

ROSEWATER FIZZ

ROSEWATER
FIZZ

—

SERVES 1

This blend of gin, rosewater and grenadine is a very pleasant way to pass time in the garden. A lovely shade of pink with an even lovelier flavour, this drink balances floral notes with pomegranate's sweet tartness. On special occasions, a rose petal or two floating on top is a simple and elegant garnish.

INGREDIENTS
...

ice cubes

1 teaspoon rosewater

25 ml (¾ fl oz) gin

25 ml (¾ fl oz) Grenadine (page 145)

chilled sparkling rose, to top

washed rose petals, to garnish

HOW TO
...

Fill a cocktail shaker with ice and add the rosewater, gin and grenadine. Shake for 30 seconds, then strain into a champagne flute and top with sparkling rose.

Garnish with rose petals.

SLOE GIN FIZZ

—

SERVES 1

Sloe gin (page 122) transforms the bite of the sloe berry into a warm and rich liqueur, reminiscent of plums. While you can purchase it ready-made at the store, it's worth the wait to prepare it yourself. If you're in a hurry, buy a bottle of liqueur to make this fizz while you wait for your gin to infuse.

INGREDIENTS
...

25 ml (¾ fl oz) Sloe gin (page 122)

1 tablespoon lemon juice

1 teaspoon Sugar syrup (page 143)

ice cubes

chilled Prosecco, to top

HOW TO
...

Combine the sloe gin, lemon juice and sugar syrup in a cocktail shaker filled with ice. Shake vigorously for 30 seconds, then strain into a champagne flute.

Top with Prosecco.

GIN-PEROL SPRITZ

—

SERVES 1

Gin, like Aperol, has enjoyed a renaissance of late. Its recent rise follows in the latter's tracks, sweeping bars and at-home liquor cabinets. This recipe marries these two mixology darlings in a quaffable blend of bittersweet and herbaceous flavours that are even tastier on an afternoon in summer.

INGREDIENTS
•••

30 ml (1 fl oz) gin

30 ml (1 fl oz) Aperol

ice cubes

60 ml (¼ cup) chilled Prosecco

chilled sparkling water

orange wheel, to garnish

3 olives on a cocktail stick, to garnish

HOW TO
•••

Combine the gin and Aperol in a large wine glass. Fill with ice.

Pour over the Prosecco and top with a dash of sparkling water. Garnish with an orange wheel and the olives.

SOUTHSIDE ROYALE

—

SERVES 1

*What makes a drink a royale? Just add bubbles.
The template originated with fruit liqueur and Champagne,
but other varieties of sparkling wine do the trick, and all sorts
of drinks benefit from a bit of carbonation. Case in point: the
Southside (page 18). With just a bit of fizz, this mint and lime
cocktail takes on a whole new class.*

INGREDIENTS
...

60 ml (¼ cup) gin

30 ml (1 fl oz) lime juice

30 ml (1 fl oz) Sugar syrup (page 143)

ice cubes

chilled sparkling white wine, to top

mint leaf, to garnish

HOW TO
...

Pour the gin, lime juice and sugar syrup into a cocktail
shaker filled with ice. Shake vigorously for 30 seconds,
then strain into a wine glass.

Top with sparkling wine and garnish with a mint leaf.

BASIL STRAWBERRY ROSE

—

SERVES 1

There are pairings that are meant to be: basil and strawberry is one. Luckily, this cocktail lets you enjoy the combination beyond summer. This drink mixes a herbaceous syrup with Strawberry gin (page 133) for a sparkling taste of warmer months that you can enjoy anytime of the year.

INGREDIENTS
...

1 tablespoon Basil syrup (page 149)

25 ml (¾ fl oz) lime juice

30 ml (1 fl oz) Strawberry gin (page 133)

ice cubes

chilled sparkling rose, to top

basil leaf, to garnish

HOW TO
...

Pour the basil syrup, lime juice and gin into a cocktail shaker filled with ice. Shake vigorously for 30 seconds, then strain into a tall glass filled with ice.

Top with sparkling rose and garnish with a basil leaf.

CUCUMBER
GIN SPRITZ

—

SERVES 1

There are few things as refreshing as a spritz. Glasses of chilled, fizzy wine mixed with aperitifs or spirits are always welcome treats to relax with – particularly when they're made with cucumber. For a bit of serenity, sip your worries away with this spritz while you lounge in some shade.

INGREDIENTS
...

30 ml (1 fl oz) gin

1 tablespoon Sugar syrup (page 143)

ice cubes

2 cucumber ribbons

125 ml (½ cup) chilled dry Prosecco

chilled sparkling water, to top

HOW TO
...

Combine the gin and sugar syrup in a cocktail shaker filled with ice. Shake for 30 seconds, then strain into a rocks glass filled with ice.

Weave the cucumber ribbons between the ice, then top with the Prosecco and a splash of sparkling water.

Bramble

Crème de Mûre

BRAMBLE

—

SERVES 1

Some things were better left in the 80s, but the bramble is not one of them. Crème de mûre lends this drink an aesthetic presence and a blackberry flavour that, paired with gin, has made it a favourite of bartenders. This version adds rosemary for an earthy twist.

INGREDIENTS

•••

1 rosemary sprig

6 blackberries

crushed ice

50 ml (1¾ fl oz) gin

20 ml (¾ fl oz) lemon juice

20 ml (¾ fl oz) Rosemary syrup (page 148)

20 ml (¾ fl oz) crème de mûre

HOW TO

•••

Remove the needles from the bottom two-thirds of the rosemary sprig, then thread 3 blackberries onto the stem. Set aside and fill a tumbler with crushed ice.

Add the gin, lemon juice, rosemary syrup and remaining blackberries to a cocktail shaker, then use a muddling tool to firmly crush the berries.

Shake for 15 seconds until well combined, then strain into the prepared tumbler. Drizzle the crème de mûre over so that it trickles down the ice, and garnish with the prepared rosemary sprig.

THAI LADY

—

SERVES 1

The aromatic presence of lemongrass plays on drinks' notes of citrus, introducing its own flavour that's reminiscent of lemon. A hint of ginger is there as well, making for a bright and refreshing addition to a glass that will transport you to a beach of white sand, if you're not already on one.

INGREDIENTS

...

ice cubes

40 ml (1¼ fl oz) gin

2 teaspoons triple sec

1 tablespoon Lemongrass syrup (page 149)

lemon wedge, to garnish

HOW TO

...

Fill a cocktail shaker with ice and add the gin, triple sec and lemongrass syrup. Shake for 30 seconds until well combined, then strain into a cocktail glass.

Serve garnished with a lemon wedge.

PINK SIPPER

—

SERVES 1

They may not be related to black peppercorns, which come from a different tree species, but pink peppercorns still taste mildly spicy. Also fruity and a touch sweet, these dried berries are a fun ingredient to experiment with in botanical cocktails. Here, they're paired with cucumber and mint for a unique herbal tipple.

INGREDIENTS

...

ice cubes

50 ml (1¾ fl oz) Cucumber & mint gin (page 121)

1 tablespoon Pink peppercorn syrup (page 148)

chilled sparkling water, to top

mint sprig, to garnish

pink peppercorns, to garnish

HOW TO

...

Place a few ice cubes in a wine glass and add the gin and peppercorn syrup.

Top with sparkling water and use a stirrer to gently swirl, then garnish with a mint sprig and a few pink peppercorns.

LAVENDER & CUCUMBER SMASH

—

SERVES 1

Spend some time in Provence during the summer, if only while you drink this smash. The lavender syrup puts the flower forward in both taste and scent. A word of warning: lavender can overpower if you use too much, so you're best to taste as you go. In the right proportions, it makes for a cocktail that's a sure crowd pleaser.

INGREDIENTS
...

1 short cucumber, peeled and roughly chopped

60 ml (¼ cup) gin

20 ml (¾ fl oz) Lavender syrup (page 147)

crushed ice

washed lavender sprig, to garnish

HOW TO
...

Put the cucumber in a blender and blitz to a fine mixture. Pass the mixture through a sieve lined with muslin (cheesecloth) into a small bowl, discarding the solids.

Pour the gin, lavender syrup and 60 ml (¼ cup) of the cucumber juice into a tumbler, and stir to combine. Top with crushed ice, and garnish with a lavender sprig.

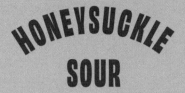

HONEYSUCKLE
SOUR

—

SERVES 1

Honeysuckle nectar is delicious, as anyone who's sampled a blossom or two in their life knows. Made into a syrup, that nectar becomes a delicate floral addition to cocktails. Just check which honeysuckle species you're using: there's more than one type climbing neighbourhood fences, and not all are edible.

INGREDIENTS
•••

ice cubes

40 ml (1¼ fl oz) tequila

20 ml (¾ fl oz) Chamomile gin (page 129)

20 ml (¾ fl oz) lime juice

50 ml (1¾ fl oz) pineapple juice

20 ml (¾ fl oz) Honeysuckle syrup (page 147)

washed honeysuckle blossom, to garnish

HOW TO
•••

Fill a cocktail shaker with ice and add the tequila, gin, lime juice, pineapple juice and honeysuckle syrup. Shake well for 30 seconds, then strain into a tall glass filled with ice.

Serve garnished with a honeysuckle blossom.

APPLE PIE

—

SERVES 1

Not quite like Grandma used to make her pies, but still a delicious way to end a meal or celebrate an occasion. Spiced gin (page 130) imbues this cocktail with a warming touch from vanilla, nutmeg and cloves. Combined with the cinnamon and sugar rim, this drink tastes just like the holidays.

INGREDIENTS
...

½ teaspoon ground cinnamon

1 tablespoon caster (superfine) sugar

lemon wedge

ice cubes

40 ml (1¼ fl oz) Spiced gin (page 130)

20 ml (¾ fl oz) vodka

20 ml (¾ fl oz) lemon juice

chilled apple cider or cloudy apple juice, to top

¼ red apple, thinly sliced, to garnish

HOW TO
...

Make a cinnamon–sugar garnish by mixing the cinnamon and sugar together on a small plate. Run a wedge of lemon around the rim of a tall glass, then press the rim into the cinnamon sugar. Fill the glass with ice.

Pour the gin, vodka and lemon juice into a cocktail shaker filled with ice. Shake well for 30 seconds, then strain into the prepared glass. Top with apple cider or juice and garnish with the apple slices.

CHAMOMILE
MARTEANI

—

SERVES 1

For those who can't choose between tea or a cocktail, just mix them together. When you'd like to wind down for the evening, a marteani is the perfect nightcap. Built with chamomile-infused gin (page 129) and honey, this one is a soothing way to end the day (or continue the evening).

INGREDIENTS
...

60 ml (¼ cup) Chamomile gin (page 129)

1 tablespoon lemon juice

20 ml (¾ fl oz) teaspoon Honey syrup (page 143)

1 egg white or 30 ml (1 fl oz) aquafaba

ice cubes

lemon twist, to garnish

HOW TO
...

Pour the gin, lemon juice, honey syrup and egg or aquafaba into a cocktail shaker and dry shake for 15 seconds. Add ice and shake for another 15 seconds.

Strain into a chilled cocktail glass and garnish with a lemon twist.

CHERRY PIE

—

Take a slice out of this cocktail – the combination of cherry gin and amaretto will have you ordering a baker's dozen. The latter's almond flavour, with its hint of cherries, rounds out this glass for the perfect after-dinner drink.

INGREDIENTS
•••

60 ml (¼ cup) Cherry gin (page 126)

2 teaspoons lemon juice

1 tablespoon amaretto

2 teaspoons Sugar syrup (page 143)

1 egg white or 30 ml (1 fl oz) aquafaba

ice cubes

Luxardo maraschino cherry, to garnish

HOW TO
•••

Add the gin, lemon juice, amaretto, sugar syrup and egg white or aquafaba to a cocktail shader, and dry shake for 15 seconds. Add ice and shake for another 15 seconds.

Strain into a tumbler and garnish with a cherry.

BREAKFAST MARTINI

BREAKFAST MARTINI

—

SERVES 1

*Marmalade is as delicious in a drink as it is spread on toast.
Its introduction to cocktails predates the modern era, but
this particular drink came into creation in the 90s. Of course,
the breakfast martini isn't really a martini at all. It is, however,
a tangy and citrusy treat worth sipping at any time of the day.*

INGREDIENTS
...

1 teaspoon good-quality orange marmalade

50 ml (1¾ fl oz) gin

1 tablespoon Grand Marnier

2 teaspoons lemon juice

2 dashes of orange bitters

ice cubes

orange twist, to garnish

HOW TO
...

Add the marmalade and gin to a cocktail shaker. Stir for
10 seconds, or until the marmalade dissolves. Add the Grand
Marnier, lemon juice, bitters and ice. Shake for 30 seconds,
then double strain into a chilled cocktail glass.

Garnish with an orange twist.

MINT SPRIG

—

SERVES 1

Grenadine (page 145) is widely relegated to Shirley Temples, but it deserves a seat at the adult table. This pomegranate syrup (no, it's not made from cherries) suits boozy drinks, as well as the mock. Here, it's a delicious partner for gin infused with cucumber and mint (page 121).

INGREDIENTS
•••

60 ml (¼ cup) Cucumber & mint gin (page 121)

30 ml (1 fl oz) lime juice

20 ml (¾ fl oz) Grenadine (page 145)

1 tablespoon Sugar syrup (page 143)

crushed ice

chilled sparkling water, to top

mint sprig, to garnish

cucumber ribbon, to garnish

HOW TO
•••

Combine the gin, lime juice, grenadine and sugar syrup in a tall glass filled with crushed ice and stir to combine.

Garnish with a mint sprig and a cucumber ribbon.

LIME BASIL SMASH

—

SERVES 1

The smash is a freewheeling form of cocktail that isn't too prescriptive when it comes to what goes in the shaker. Whatever pours out is usually a combination of something fresh and something alcoholic. In this case, basil and lime are mixed with gin for an aromatic, icy treat.

INGREDIENTS
...

zest of 1 lime

1 tablespoon caster (superfine) sugar

lime wedge

ice cubes

about 10 basil leaves, plus a sprig to garnish

60 ml (¼ cup) gin

20 ml (¾ fl oz) lime juice

1 tablespoon Sugar syrup (page 143)

HOW TO
...

Make a lime–sugar garnish by mixing the lime zest and sugar together on a small plate. Run a wedge of lime around the rim of a rocks glass, then press the rim into the lime sugar. Fill the glass with ice.

Place the basil in a cocktail shaker and muddle gently, then add the gin, lime juice and sugar syrup. Fill the shaker with ice and shake for 30 seconds, until well combined.

Strain into the prepared glass and garnish with a basil sprig.

AMERICANO FIZZ

—

SERVES 1

*The Americano: as the story goes, the drink that inspired the Negroni (page 21), and as **Casino Royale** goes, the very first cocktail James Bond orders. A bartending classic, it's a delicious blend of vermouth and Campari topped off with sparkling water. This fizz takes things further with the addition of gin and a frothy finish. Not what Bond orders, but certainly worth mixing.*

INGREDIENTS

...

45 ml (1½ fl oz) sweet vermouth

45 ml (1½ fl oz) Campari

25 ml (¾ fl oz) gin

1 egg white or 30 ml (1 fl oz) aquafaba

ice cubes

chilled sparkling water, to top

orange wheel, to garnish

HOW TO

...

Pour the vermouth, Campari, gin and egg white or aquafaba into a cocktail shaker filled with ice. Dry shake for 15 seconds, then add ice and shake for another 15 seconds. Strain into a tall glass filled with ice and top with sparkling water.

Garnish with an orange wheel.

GIN-GIN MULE

—

SERVES 1

A drink created in the 21st century. While the gin-gin mule is newer than many other cocktails, it belongs to an older tradition. This mule takes after both the mojito and the Moscow mule, combining ginger, gin and mint for an incredibly refreshing New York-born creation.

INGREDIENTS
...

10 mint leaves, plus a sprig to garnish

2 teaspoons Sugar syrup (page 143)

20 ml (¾ fl oz) lime juice

60 ml (¼ cup) gin

ice cubes

chilled ginger beer, to top

HOW TO
...

In a cocktail shaker, gently muddle the mint leaves, sugar syrup and lime juice. Add the gin and ice, and shake for 30 seconds.

Strain into a tall glass filled with ice, top with ginger beer and garnish with a mint sprig.

INFUSIONS

BLUE FLORAL GIN

—

MAKES 750 ML (3 CUPS)

If you want to improve your bartending flair, try this recipe. Gin infused with butterfly pea flowers takes on a vibrant blue hue, until you add an acid: that blue then morphs into a rich purple. As colourful as this gin is, though, the flowers only impart a tinge of flavour, which means this infusion suits plenty of cocktails.

INGREDIENTS

•••

4–6 washed lavender sprigs, flowers picked

1 tablespoon dried edible butterfly pea flowers

750 ml (3 cups) gin

HOW TO

•••

Place the lavender flowers in a clean jar or container with a lid (page 11). Add the butterfly pea flowers and gin, then cover with the lid and shake gently.

Leave to infuse for 2–3 hours, then taste – the flavours will get stronger the longer you leave them to infuse.

Pass the gin through a sieve lined with muslin (cheesecloth) into a jug, discarding the solids. Transfer to a clean bottle or jar, seal and use as desired.

CUCUMBER & MINT GIN

CUCUMBER & MINT GIN

—

MAKES 750 ML (3 CUPS)

When it comes to ingredients, there are few as cool or rejuvenating as mint and cucumber. Partnered together, they're an unbeatable combo that produces a thirst-quenching gin. Add ice and a splash of sparkling water, and you'll be set for the day's refreshments.

INGREDIENTS
...

1 long cucumber, peeled, seeded and sliced

1 small bunch mint

750 ml (3 cups) gin

HOW TO
...

Place the cucumber and mint in a clean 1 litre (4 cup) capacity jar or container with a lid (page 11). Pour in the gin, ensuring the cucumber and mint are fully submerged. Cover with the lid and shake gently.

Leave the jar in a cool, dark place for 1–2 days, gently shaking each day. Taste the infusion to check if you are happy with the flavour, leaving for longer if you want a stronger flavour.

Pass the gin through a sieve lined with muslin (cheesecloth) into a jug, discarding the solids. Transfer to a clean bottle or jar, seal and use as desired.

SLOE GIN

—

MAKES 750 ML (3 CUPS)

While you start with gin, you end with a liqueur when you infuse the spirit with sloe berries and sugar. The process cuts the alcohol content and sweetens the gin, until you have a lower-proof, ruby-red bottle that tastes much better than the raw berries. You can try one pre-steeping, but don't say that you weren't warned.

INGREDIENTS

...

500 g (1 lb 2 oz) sloe berries

750 ml (3 cups) gin

215 g (7½ oz) caster (superfine) sugar

HOW TO

...

Place the sloe berries in a clean 1 litre (4 cup) capacity jar or container with a lid (see page 11). Gently muddle the berries, then add the gin and sugar, ensuring the fruit is fully submerged. Cover with the lid and shake gently.

Leave the jar in a cool, dark place for 3 months, gently shaking every other day. Taste the infusion to check if you are happy with the flavour, leaving for longer if you want a stronger flavour.

Pass the liqueur through a sieve lined with muslin (cheesecloth) into a jug, discarding the solids. Transfer to a clean bottle or jar, seal and use as desired.

VANILLA + PEAR
GIN

VANILLA & PEAR GIN

—

MAKES 750 ML (3 CUPS)

When it comes to which pears to use in this infusion, you have your pick of varieties. Whichever you choose, vanilla is a great match. A popular addition to infused gins, just a touch of vanilla adds a warm, sweet touch that complements pear's crispness.

INGREDIENTS
...

3–4 small pears, quartered and cored

750 ml (3 cups) gin

1 vanilla bean, split lengthways

HOW TO
...

Place the pear in a clean 1 litre (4 cup) capacity jar or container with a lid (see page 11). Pour in the gin, ensuring the fruit is fully submerged. Cover with the lid and shake gently.

Leave the jar in a cool, dark place for 4 days, gently shaking each day. On the fourth day, add the vanilla bean to the jar, then cover again and shake. Leave for 3–4 more days, tasting daily until you are happy with the flavour.

Pass the gin through a sieve lined with muslin (cheesecloth) into a jug, discarding the solids. Transfer to a clean bottle or jar, seal and use as desired.

CHERRY GIN

—

MAKES 750 ML (3 CUPS)

While cherries aren't in season forever, you can enjoy their taste well past summer. Infused in gin, they impart a rich colour and flavour. This warm, sweet liquor is very mixable: try it with tonic, use it in a Martinez (page 34) or sip it on its own over ice. It won't be hard to find the bottom of your supply.

INGREDIENTS
...

450 g (1 lb) cherries, pitted and quartered

750 ml (3 cups) gin

115 g (½ cup) caster (superfine) sugar

HOW TO
...

Place the cherries in a clean 1 litre (4 cup) capacity jar or container with a lid (see page 11) and muddle them. Add the gin and sugar, ensuring the fruit is fully submerged. Cover with the lid and shake gently.

Leave the jar in a cool, dark place for 1 week, gently shaking each day. Taste the infusion to check if you are happy with the flavour, leaving for longer if you want a stronger flavour.

Pass the gin through a sieve lined with muslin (cheesecloth) into a jug, discarding the solids. Transfer to a clean bottle or jar, seal and use as desired.

CHAMOMILE GIN

—

MAKES 750 ML (3 CUPS)

When you want to relax, chamomile's calming touch is just the answer. With a gentle flavour, the flowers don't overpower the gin. Instead, they add a subtle note of fruity and floral sweetness. Try this gin in drinks with honey, and you'll sip the day right away.

INGREDIENTS

...

½ cup dried edible chamomile flowers

750 ml (3 cups) gin

HOW TO

...

Place the flowers and gin in a clean 1 litre (4 cup) capacity jar or container with a lid (see page 11). Cover with the lid and shake gently.

Taste the infusion after 1–2 days to check if you are happy with the flavour, leaving for longer if you want a stronger flavour.

Pass the gin through a sieve lined with muslin (cheesecloth) into a jug, discarding the solids. Transfer to a clean bottle or jar, seal and use as desired.

SPICED GIN

—

MAKES 750 ML (3 CUPS)

A gin for colder weather. Spices like cinnamon and cloves will warm you from belly to mittens, with a taste that's reminiscent of the holiday season. If you're feeling adventurous, add your own spices for a personalised bottle of gin that's perfect to gift – or to keep for yourself.

INGREDIENTS
...

2 strips of orange peel

1 cinnamon stick

4 cloves

1 vanilla bean, split lengthways

¼ teaspoon nutmeg

750 ml (3 cups) gin

HOW TO
...

Place the orange peel and spices in a clean 1 litre (4 cup) capacity jar or container with a lid (see page 11). Pour in the gin, cover with the lid and shake gently.

Leave the jar in a cool, dark place for 3–4 days, gently shaking each day. Taste the infusion to check if you are happy with the flavour, leaving for longer if you want a stronger flavour.

Pass the gin through a sieve lined with muslin (cheesecloth) into a jug, discarding the solids. Transfer to a clean bottle or jar, seal and use as desired.

STRAWBERRY GIN

STRAWBERRY GIN

—

MAKES 750 ML (3 CUPS)

When the garden's ripe and bursting, chuck a few of your strawberries into some gin. After a few days, the results will be juicy and ready to add a bright note to your cocktails. Strawberries make a great partner for herbs like basil – try it in cocktails with a few muddled leaves, or in fruitier concoctions for something sweeter.

INGREDIENTS
•••

250 g (9 oz) strawberries, hulled and quartered

750 ml (3 cups) gin

HOW TO
•••

Place the strawberries in a clean 1 litre (4 cup) capacity jar or container with a lid (see page 11). Pour in the gin, ensuring the fruit is fully submerged. Cover with the lid and shake gently.

Place the jar in a cool, dark place for 2–3 days, gently shaking each day. Taste the infusion to check if you are happy with the flavour, leaving for longer if you want a stronger flavour.

Pass the gin through a sieve lined with muslin (cheesecloth) into a jug, discarding the solids. Transfer to a clean bottle or jar, seal and use as desired.

COMPOUND GIN

—

MAKES 750 ML (3 CUPS)

While it might be quicker to simply buy a ready-made gin, creating your own by infusing botanicals in vodka is a fun experiment. Alcohol created this way is also called 'bathtub gin', but I wouldn't advise dipping anything other than garnishes in it. If you're feeling adventurous, try your own blends of aromatics and see what happens.

INGREDIENTS
...

3 tablespoons juniper berries

750 ml (3 cups) vodka

2 strips of orange peel

4 cardamom pods

4 allspice berries

1 bay leaf

¼ teaspoon black pepper

1 teaspoon coriander seeds

HOW TO
...

Place the juniper berries in a clean 1 litre (4 cup) capacity jar or container with a lid (see page 11). Gently muddle them, then add the citrus peel, spices and vodka, ensuring the fruit is fully submerged. Cover with the lid and shake gently.

Leave the jar in a cool, dark place for 4–5 days, gently shaking each day. Taste the infusion to check if you are happy with the flavour, leaving for longer if you want a stronger flavour.

Pass the gin through a sieve lined with muslin (cheesecloth) into a jug, discarding the solids. Transfer to a clean bottle or jar, seal and use as desired.

·CITRUS·GIN·

CITRUS GIN

—

MAKES 750 ML (3 CUPS)

Besides alcohol, there are few ingredients as key to bartending as citrus. Without limes and lemons, many cocktails would no longer exist: the Gin Rickey (page 29). The Gimlet (page 26). The world and our bars would be sadder places. Luckily, we have our pick of citrus to infuse into gin, from mandarins to yuzus. Feel free to mix and match your favourites.

INGREDIENTS
•••

2 lemons

1 orange or blood orange

750 ml (3 cups) gin

HOW TO
•••

Wash the lemons and orange, then use a vegetable peeler to peel the zest from the fruit, leaving behind as much of the white pith as you can manage. Keep the rest of the fruit for another use. Place the zest in a clean 1 litre (4 cup) capacity jar or container with a lid (see page 11). Pour in the gin, ensuring the zest is fully submerged. Cover with the lid and shake gently.

Leave the jar in a cool, dark place for 5 days, gently shaking each day. Taste the infusion to check if you are happy with the flavour, leaving for longer if you want a stronger flavour.

Pass the gin through a sieve lined with muslin (cheesecloth) into a jug, discarding the solids. Transfer to a clean bottle or jar, seal and use as desired.

RASPBERRY GIN

—

MAKES 750 ML (3 CUPS)

A fruity gin for those who like a bit of tartness. Raspberries suit plenty of cocktails, from the Gin fizz (page 30) to the Gimlet (page 26) and the Breakfast martini (page 107). The berry's notes are widely complementary; experiment with your favourite drinks, create new ones and sample them on a sunny day in the garden.

INGREDIENTS
...

375 g (13 oz) raspberries

750 ml (3 cups) gin

HOW TO
...

Place the raspberries in a clean 1 litre (4 cup) capacity jar or container with a lid (see page 11). Gently muddle the berries, then pour in the gin, ensuring the fruit is fully submerged. Cover with the lid and shake gently.

Leave the jar in a cool, dark place for 5–7 days, gently shaking each day. Taste the infusion to check if you are happy with the flavour, leaving for longer if you want a stronger flavour.

Pass the gin through a sieve lined with muslin (cheesecloth) into a jug, discarding the solids. Transfer to a clean bottle or jar, seal and use as desired.

RASPBERRY GIN

SYRUPS

YOU CAN PURCHASE MANY READY-MADE SYRUPS IF YOU DON'T WANT TO PREPARE THEM FROM SCRATCH, BUT HOMEMADE SYRUPS REQUIRE VERY LITTLE KNOW-HOW OR INGREDIENTS.

Once you get the hang of making your own syrups, a world of new cocktails opens up. When it comes to flavours, the possibilities are endless; mix and match your favourites to make unique tipples, and experiment with different botanicals to see how they interact with your gin. Like infusions, syrups are a great opportunity to get creative behind the bar.

SUGAR

—

INGREDIENTS
...

110 g (4 oz) caster
(superfine) sugar

HOW TO
...

Combine the sugar and 125 ml
(½ cup) of water in a small
saucepan. Bring to the boil and stir
until the sugar dissolves. Remove
from the heat and allow to cool.

The sugar syrup will keep in an
airtight container in the fridge
for up to 1 week.

HONEY

—

MAKES 125 ML (½ CUP)

INGREDIENTS
...

90 g (3 oz) honey

1¼ tablespoons chilli
flakes (optional)

1 tablespoon apple cider
vinegar (optional)

HOW TO
...

Combine the honey and 90 ml
(3 fl oz) of water in a small
saucepan over low heat. Stir until
the honey dissolves. Set aside
to cool.

To make a hot honey syrup, add
the chilli flakes and vinegar. If you
like milder spice, pass the syrup
through a sieve lined with muslin
(cheesecloth) into a container after
10 minutes, discarding the solids.
If you like your honey hot, leave the
chilli flakes in.

The honey syrup will keep in an
airtight container in the fridge for
up to 1 week.

LIME

—

MAKES 55 ML (1¾ FL OZ)

INGREDIENTS
...

55 g (¼ cup) caster (superfine) sugar

zest and juice of 1 lime

HOW TO
...

Combine the sugar, zest and 125 ml (½ cup) of water in a small saucepan. Bring to the boil and stir until the sugar dissolves. Remove from the heat and add the juice, then set aside for 30 minutes to infuse. Strain through a fine-mesh sieve into a container, discarding the solids.

The lime syrup will keep in an airtight container in the fridge for up to 1 week.

RASPBERRY

—

MAKES 60 ML (¼ CUP)

INGREDIENTS
...

55 g (¼ cup) caster (superfine) sugar

5 raspberries

HOW TO
...

Combine the sugar and 60 ml (¼ cup) of water in a small saucepan. Bring to the boil and stir until the sugar dissolves. Remove from the heat and add the raspberries, using a fork to crush them. Set aside to infuse for an hour, then pass through a fine-mesh sieve into a container, discarding the solids.

The raspberry syrup will keep in an airtight container in the fridge for up to 5 days.

GRENADINE

—

MAKES 60 ML (¼ CUP)

INGREDIENTS
...

60 ml (¼ cup) pomegranate juice

30 g (1 oz) caster (superfine) sugar

2 teaspoons lemon juice

HOW TO
...

In a small saucepan, bring the pomegranate juice to the boil and simmer until reduced by half. Add the sugar and stir until dissolved, then add the lemon juice. Remove from the heat and allow to cool.

The grenadine will keep in an airtight container in the fridge for up to 1 week.

ROSE PETAL

—

MAKES 115 ML (4 FL OZ)

INGREDIENTS
...

½ cup dried edible rose petals

115 g (½ cup) caster (superfine) sugar

HOW TO
...

Combine the rose petals, sugar and 125 ml (½ cup) of water in a small saucepan. Bring to the boil and stir until the sugar dissolves. Remove from the heat and leave to cool, then refrigerate for 4 hours, or overnight for a stronger flavour. Strain into a container, discarding the solids.

The rose petal syrup will keep in an airtight container in the fridge for 4–5 days.

LILAC

—

MAKES 55 ML (1¾ FL OZ)

INGREDIENTS

···

55 g (¼ cup) caster
(superfine) sugar

2 teaspoons washed lilac florets
(purple flowers only)

HOW TO

···

Combine the sugar and 60 ml
(¼ cup) of water in a small
saucepan. Bring to the boil and stir
until the sugar dissolves. Add the
lilac and simmer for 1–2 minutes.
Remove from the heat and leave
to cool, then transfer to an airtight
container and leave to infuse for
4 hours or overnight in the fridge.
Strain into a container, discarding
the solids.

The lilac syrup will keep in an
airtight container in the fridge
for 4–5 days.

PANSY

—

MAKES 55 ML (1¾ FL OZ)

INGREDIENTS

···

55 g (¼ cup) caster
(superfine) sugar

5–6 washed pansies

HOW TO

···

Combine the sugar and 60 ml
(¼ cup) of water in a small
saucepan. Bring to the boil and
stir until the sugar dissolves.
Place the pansies in a heatproof
container and pour over the syrup.
Mix, then cover and leave to infuse
overnight in the fridge. Strain into
a container, discarding the solids.

The pansy syrup will keep in an
airtight container in the fridge
for 4–5 days.

HONEYSUCKLE

—

MAKES 205–235 ML (7–8 FL OZ)

INGREDIENTS

...

1 cup washed honeysuckle petals, green parts and leaves removed

250 ml (1 cup) near-boiling water

170–230 g (¾–1 cup) caster (superfine) sugar

HOW TO

...

Combine the honeysuckle and water in a heatproof container. Stir well, then cover and leave to infuse in the fridge overnight.

Pass the mixture through a sieve lined with muslin (cheesecloth) into a measuring jug, discarding the solids. Add an equal measure of sugar, then transfer to a small saucepan. Bring to the boil and stir until the sugar dissolves, then remove from the heat and allow to cool.

The honeysuckle syrup will keep in an airtight container in the fridge for up to 1 week.

LAVENDER

—

MAKES 55 ML (1¾ FL OZ)

INGREDIENTS

...

55 g (¼ cup) caster (superfine) sugar

2–3 teaspoons dried edible lavender flowers

HOW TO

...

Combine the sugar, 2 teaspoons of the dried lavender and 60 ml (¼ cup) of water in a small saucepan – add an extra teaspoon of lavender for a stronger taste. Bring to the boil and stir until the sugar dissolves. Remove from the heat and set aside for 30 minutes to infuse. Strain through a fine-mesh sieve into a container, discarding the solids.

The lavender syrup will keep in an airtight container in the fridge for 4–5 days.

PINK PEPPERCORN

—

MAKES 55 ML (1¾ FL OZ)

INGREDIENTS
...

55 g (¼ cup) caster
(superfine) sugar

2–3 teaspoons pink peppercorns

HOW TO
...

Combine the sugar, 2 teaspoons
of the pink peppercorns and
60 ml (¼ cup) of water in a
small saucepan – add an extra
teaspoon of peppercorns if you
want more of a kick. Bring to
the boil and stir until the sugar
dissolves. Remove from the heat
and set aside for 30 minutes to
infuse. Strain through a fine-
mesh sieve into a container,
discarding the solids.

The remaining peppercorn syrup
will keep in an airtight container in
the fridge for 4–5 days.

ROSEMARY

—

MAKES 55 ML (1¾ FL OZ)

INGREDIENTS
...

2 rosemary sprigs, leaves picked
and roughly chopped

55 g (¼ cup) caster
(superfine) sugar

HOW TO
...

Combine the rosemary, sugar and
60 ml (¼ cup) of water in a small
saucepan. Bring to the boil and stir
until the sugar dissolves. Remove
from the heat and leave to infuse
for 30 minutes. Pass the syrup
through a sieve lined with muslin
(cheesecloth) into a container,
discarding the solids.

The rosemary syrup will keep in
an airtight container in the fridge
for 4–5 days.

LEMONGRASS

—

MAKES 115 ML (4 FL OZ)

INGREDIENTS

...

115 g (½ cup) caster
(superfine) sugar

1 lemongrass stalk, white part
only, chopped

HOW TO

...

Combine the sugar, lemongrass
and 125 ml (½ cup) of water in
a small saucepan. Bring to the boil
and stir until the sugar dissolves,
then leave to simmer for about
5 minutes. Remove from the
heat, leave to cool and transfer
to the fridge to infuse overnight.
Strain into a container, discarding
the solids.

The lemongrass syrup will keep in
an airtight container in the fridge
for 4–5 days.

BASIL

—

MAKES 55 ML (1¾ FL OZ)

INGREDIENTS

...

55 g (¼ cup) caster
(superfine) sugar

½ bunch basil, leaves picked

HOW TO

...

Combine the sugar, basil and 60 ml
(¼ cup) of water in a saucepan.
Bring to the boil and stir until
the sugar dissolves. Remove
from the heat and set aside for
30 minutes to infuse. Strain into
a container, discarding the solids.

The basil syrup will keep in an
airtight container in the fridge
for 4–5 days.

INDEX

—

Smith Street Books

Published in 2023 by Smith Street Books
Naarm (Melbourne) | Australia
smithstreetbooks.com

ISBN: 978-1-9227-5448-6

Smith Street Books respectfully acknowledges the Wurundjeri
People of the Kulin Nation, who are the Traditional Owners of
the land on which we work, and we pay our respects to their
Elders past and present.

Publisher: Paul McNally
Editor and text: Avery Hayes
Designer, illustrator and typesetter: Anna Manolatos
Proofreader: Ariana Klepac
Indexer: Helena Holmgren

Printed & bound in China by C&C Offset Printing Co., Ltd.

Book 281
10 9 8 7 6 5 4 3 2 1

MIX
Paper | Supporting
responsible forestry
FSC® C008047
FSC
www.fsc.org